Impressum
Verlag: BABADADA GmbH, Nedderfeld 112 , 22529 Hamburg
Geschäftsführer / Verlagsleitung: Harald Hof
Druck: Books on Demand GmbH, In de Tarpen 42, 22848 Norderstedt

Imprint
Publisher: BABADADA GmbH, Nedderfeld 112 , 22529 Hamburg, Germany
Managing Director / Publishing direction: Harald Hof
Print: Books on Demand GmbH, In de Tarpen 42, 22848 Norderstedt

学校

school

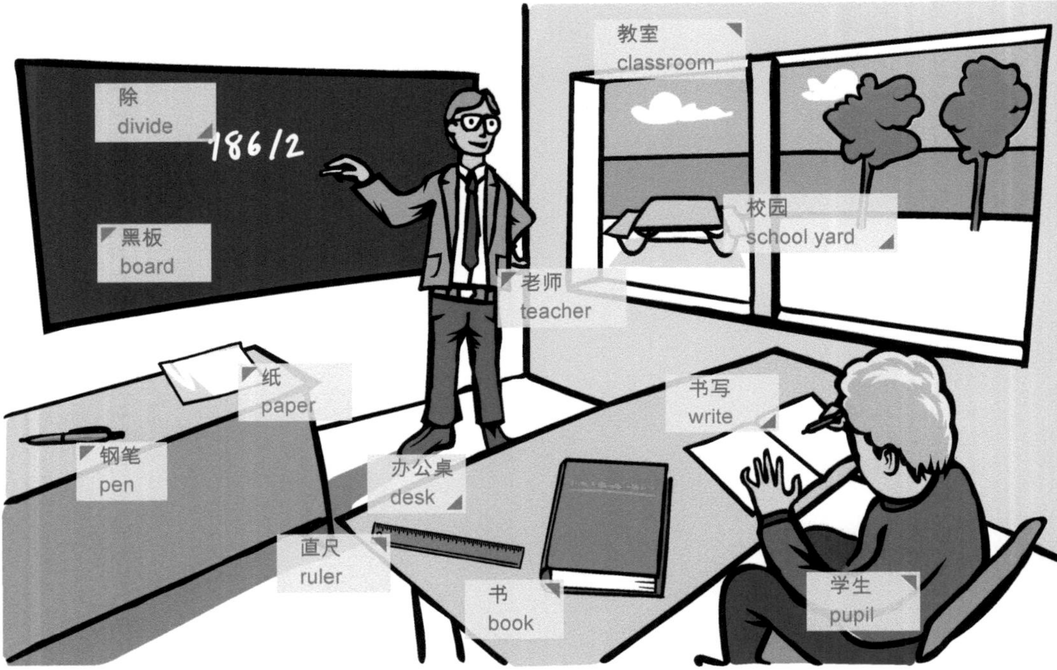

教室
classroom
除
divide
186/2
黑板
board
校园
school yard
老师
teacher
纸
paper
书写
write
钢笔
pen
办公桌
desk
直尺
ruler
书
book
学生
pupil

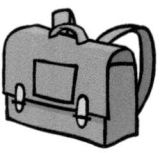

书包

satchel

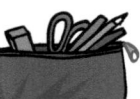

铅笔盒

pencil case

铅笔

pencil

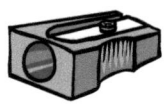

卷笔刀

pencil sharpener

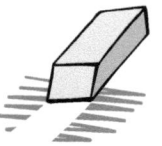

橡皮擦

rubber

画板

drawing pad

图画
drawing

画笔
paintbrush

颜料盒
paint box

剪刀
scissors

胶水
glue

练习册
exercise book

家庭作业
homework

12

数字
number

2+2

加
add

5-2

减
subtract

2×2

乘
multiply

计算
calculate

A

字母
letter

ABCDEFG
HIJKLMN
OPQRSTU
VWXYZ

字母表
alphabet

hello

字
word

课文

text

读

read

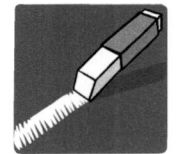

粉笔

chalk

上课

lesson

登记

register

考试

exam

证书

certificate

校服

school uniform

教育

education

百科全书

encyclopedia

大学

university

显微镜

microscope

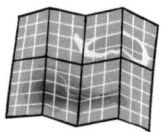

地图

map

废纸筐

waste-paper basket

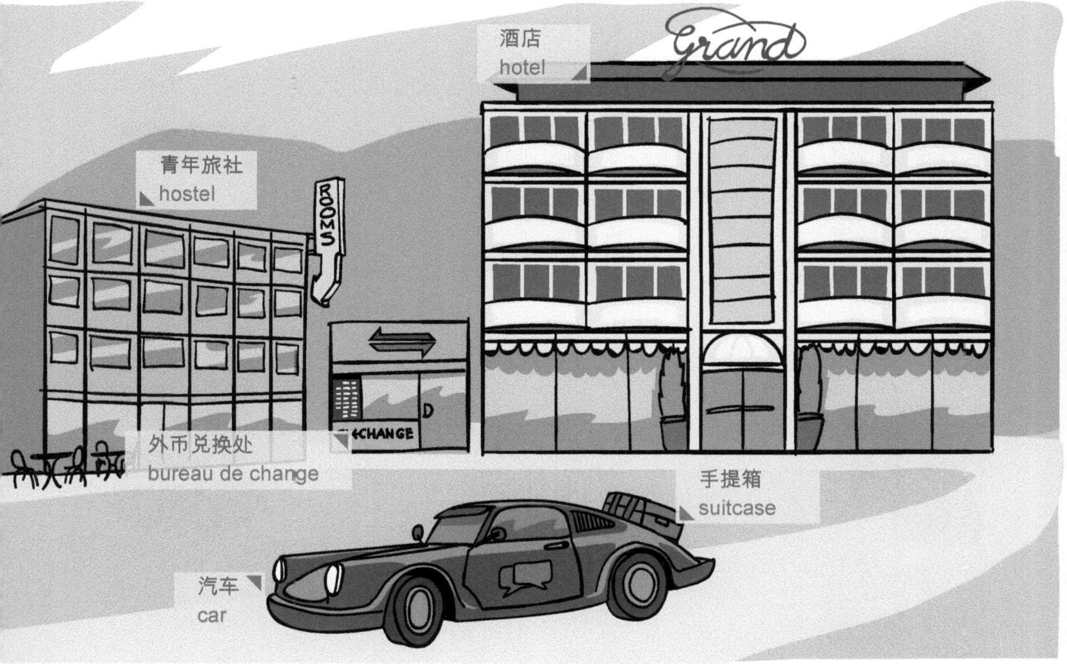
酒店
hotel
Grand
青年旅社
hostel
ROOMS
外币兑换处
bureau de change
手提箱
suitcase
汽车
car

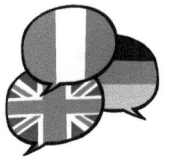

语言

language

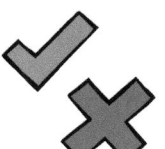

是/否

yes / no

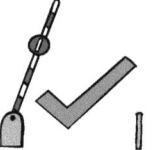

好的

Okay

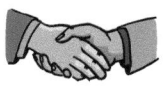

您好

hello

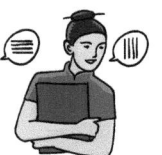

翻译员

translator

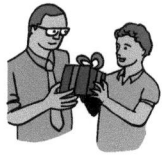

谢谢

Thank you

......多少钱？

how much is...?

我不明白

I do not understand

问题

problem

晚上好！

Good evening!

早上好！

Good morning!

晚安！

Good night!

再见

bye bye

方向

direction

行李

luggage

包

bag

双肩包

backpack

客人

guest

房间

room

睡袋

sleeping bag

帐篷

tent

旅游信息

tourist information

海滩

beach

信用卡

credit card

早餐

breakfast

午餐

lunch

晚餐

dinner

票

ticket

电梯

lift

邮票

stamp

边界

border

海关

customs

大使馆

embassy

签证

visa

护照

passport

交通运输

transport

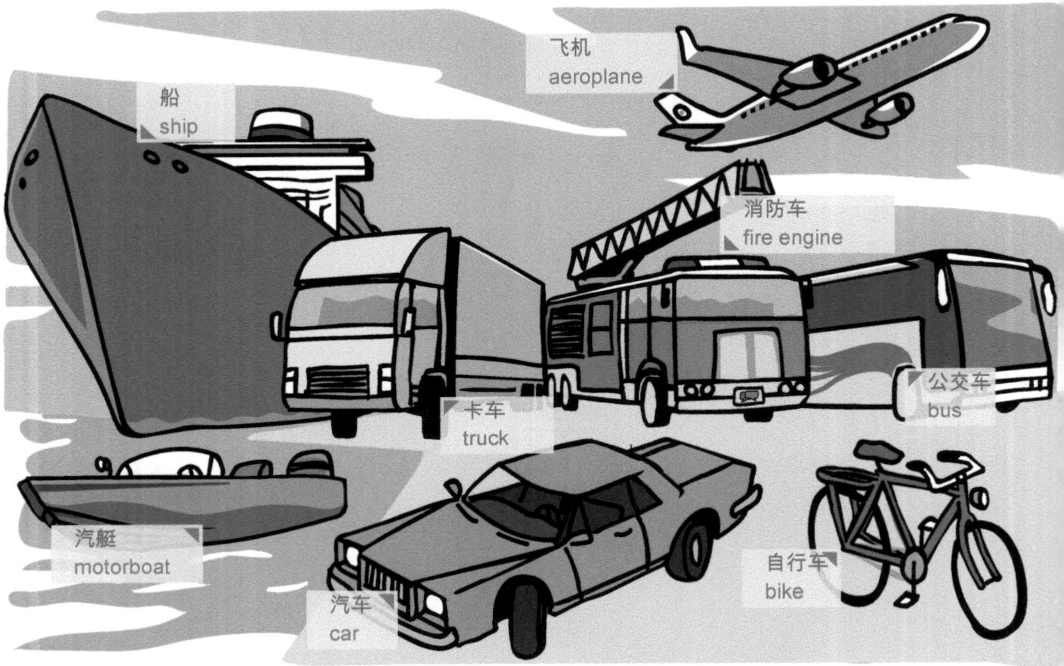

飞机
aeroplane
船
ship
消防车
fire engine
公交车
bus
卡车
truck
汽艇
motorboat
自行车
bike
汽车
car

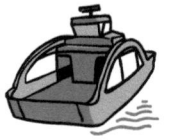

摆渡船

ferry

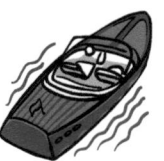

小船

boat

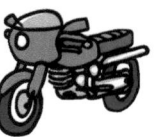

摩托车

motorbike

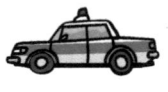

警车

police car

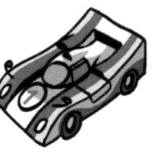

赛车

racing car

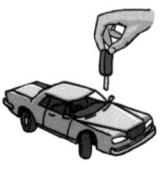

租车

rental car

拼车

car sharing

拖车

breakdown truck

垃圾车

refuse truck

发动机

motor

汽油

fuel

加油站

petrol station

交通标志

traffic sign

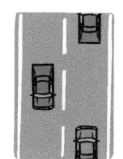

交通

traffic

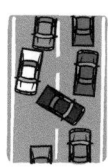

交通堵塞

traffic jam

停车场

car park

火车站

train station

轨道

tracks

火车

train

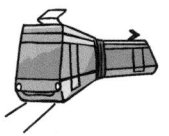

电车

tram

货车

carriage

直升机

helicopter

机场

airport

塔

tower

乘客

passenger

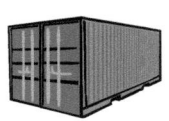

集装箱

container

纸板箱

carton

手推车

cart

篮子

basket

起飞/降落

take off / land

城市

city

村庄

village

市中心

city centre

房子

house

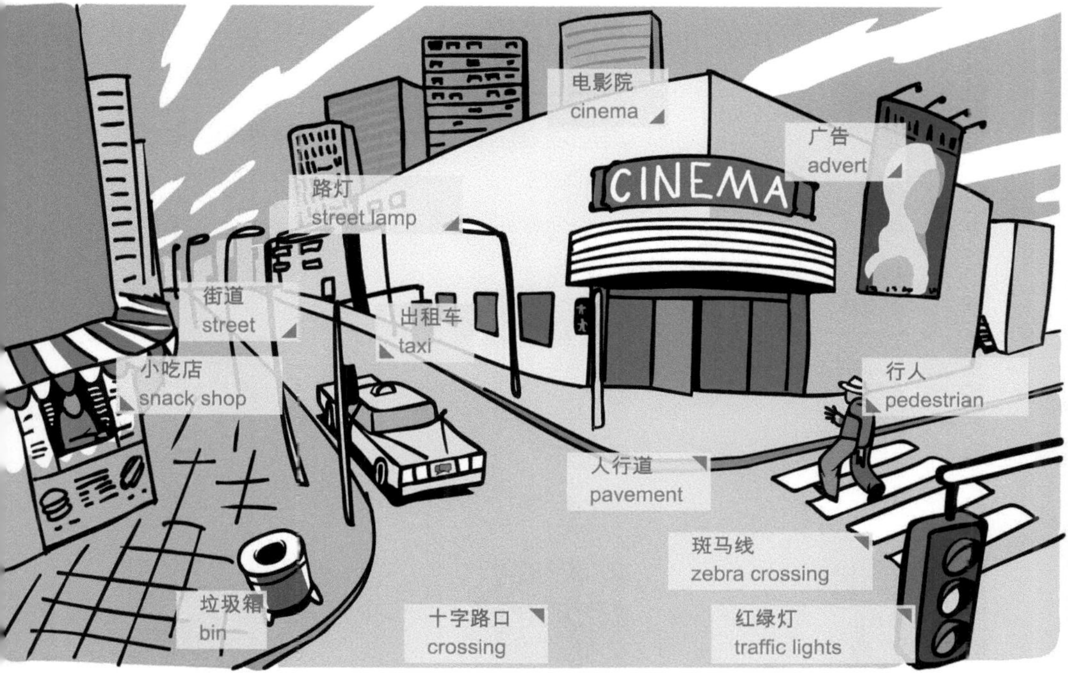

电影院
cinema
CINEMA
广告
advert
路灯
street lamp
街道
street
出租车
taxi
小吃店
snack shop
行人
pedestrian
人行道
pavement
斑马线
zebra crossing
垃圾箱
bin
十字路口
crossing
红绿灯
traffic lights

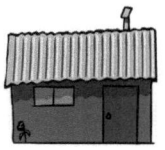

小屋

hut

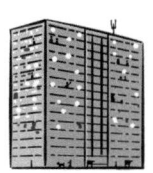

公寓

flat

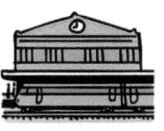

火车站

train station

市政厅

town hall

MUSEUM

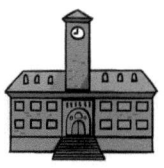

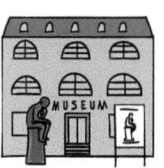

博物馆

museum

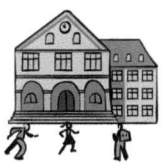

学校

school

大学

university

银行

bank

医院

hospital

酒店

hotel

药房

pharmacy

办公室

office

书店

book shop

商店

shop

花店

florist's

超市

supermarket

市场

market

百货商店

department store

鱼店

fishmonger's

购物中心

shopping centre

海港

harbour

公园

park

长凳

bench

桥

bridge

楼梯

stairs

地铁

underground

隧道

tunnel

公交车站

bus stop

酒吧

bar

餐馆

restaurant

邮筒

postbox

路标

street sign

停车计时器

parking meter

动物园

zoo

游泳馆

swimming pool

清真寺

mosque

农场
farm

污染
pollution

基地
graveyard

教堂
church

操场
playground

寺庙
temple

地形
landscape

树叶
leaf

指示牌
signpost

路
way

草地
meadow

石头
stone

树
tree

徒步旅行
者
hiker

河
river

草
grass

花
flower

峡谷
valley

山
hill

湖
lake

森林
forest

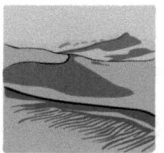
沙漠
desert

火山
volcano

城堡
castle

彩虹
rainbow

蘑菇
mushroom

棕榈树
palm tree

蚊子
mosquito

苍蝇
fly

蚂蚁
ant

蜜蜂
bee

蜘蛛
spider

甲虫

beetle

青蛙

frog

松鼠

squirrel

刺猬

hedgehog

野兔

hare

猫头鹰

owl

鸟

bird

天鹅

swan

野猪

boar

鹿

deer

麋鹿

moose

水坝

dam

风力发电机

wind turbine

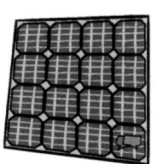

太阳能电池板

solar panel

气候

climate

餐馆

restaurant

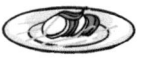

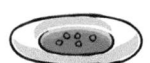

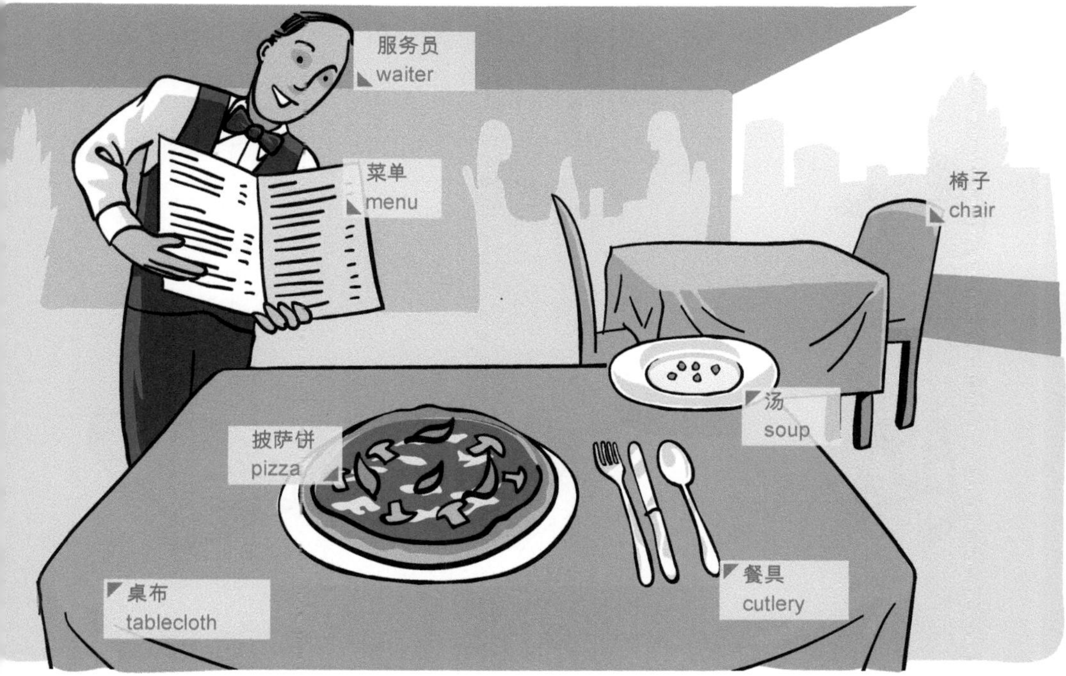

服务员
waiter
菜单
menu
椅子
chair
汤
soup
披萨饼
pizza
餐具
cutlery
桌布
tablecloth

前菜

starter

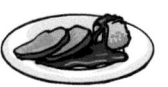

主菜

main course

甜点

dessert

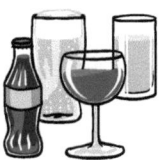

饮料

drinks

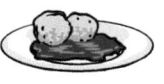

食物

food

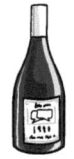

瓶子

bottle

快餐

fast food

街边小吃

street food

茶壶

teapot

糖盒

sugar bowl

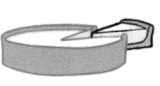

一份饭菜

portion

意式咖啡机

espresso machine

高脚椅

high chair

账单

bill

托盘

tray

刀

knife

餐叉

fork

勺子

spoon

茶匙

teaspoon

餐巾

serviette

玻璃杯

glass

碟子
plate

汤盘
soup plate

碟子
saucer

酱
sauce

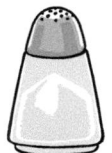

盐瓶
salt pot

胡椒磨
pepper mill

醋
vinegar

食用油
oil

调味料
spices

番茄酱
ketchup

芥末
mustard

蛋黄酱
mayonnaise

超市

supermarket

特价
special offer
FOR
顾客
customer
乳制品
dairy
水果
fruit
购物车
trolley

BUTCHERS

肉铺

butcher´s

BAKERY

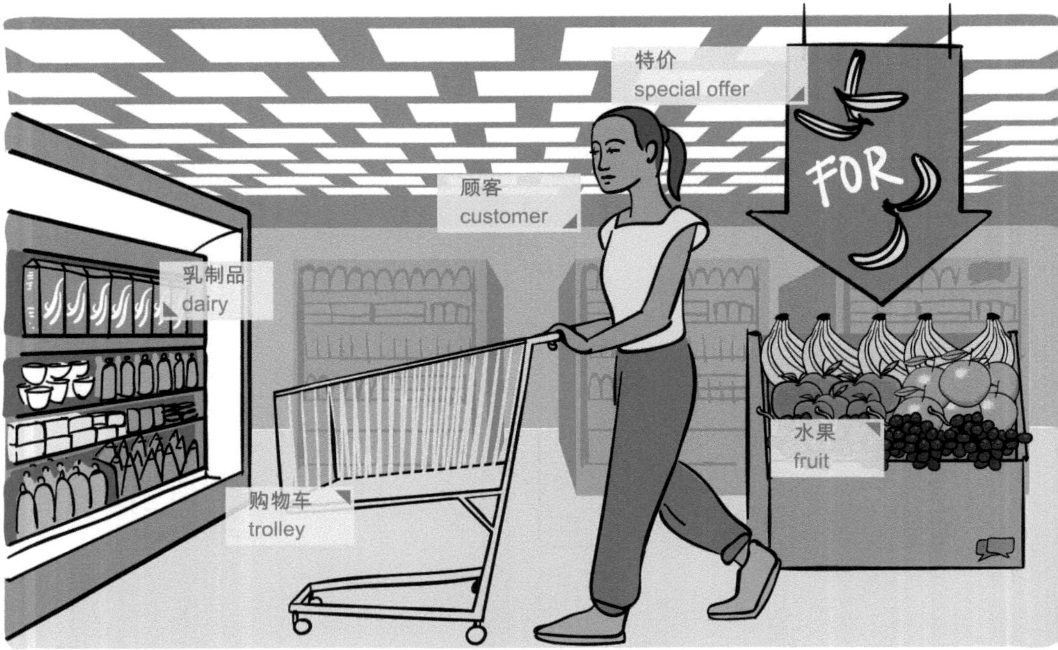

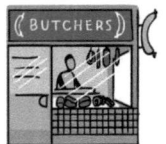

面包房

baker´s

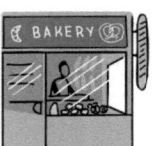

称重

weigh

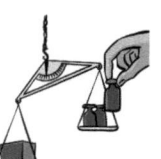

蔬菜

vegetables

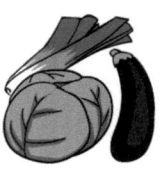

肉

meat

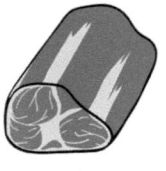

冷冻食品

frozen food

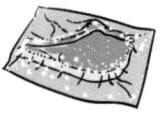

冷盘
cold meat

罐头食品
tinned food

洗衣粉
washing powder

甜食
sweets

日用品
household products

清洁用品
cleaning products

销售员
salesperson

收银机
till

收银员
cashier

购物清单
shopping list

开放时间
opening hours

钱包
wallet

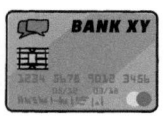

信用卡
credit card

袋子
bag

塑料袋
plastic bag

水

water

果汁

juice

牛奶

milk

可乐

coke

红酒

wine

啤酒

beer

酒

alcohol

可可

cocoa

茶

tea

咖啡

coffee

意式浓缩咖啡

espresso

卡布奇诺

cappuccino

香蕉

banana

苹果

apple

橙子

orange

西瓜

melon

柠檬

lemon

胡萝卜

carrot

大蒜

garlic

竹子

bamboo

洋葱

onion

蘑菇

mushroom

坚果

nuts

面条

noodles

意大利面条

spaghetti

米饭

rice

沙拉

salad

薯条

chips

炸土豆

fried potatoes

披萨饼

pizza

汉堡包

hamburger

三明治

sandwich

炸猪排

cutlet

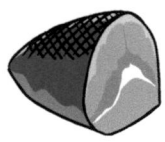

火腿

ham

萨拉米

salami

香肠

sausage

鸡肉

chicken

烤肉

roast

鱼

fish

燕麦片
porridge oats

穆兹利
muesli

玉米片
cornflakes

面粉
flour

croissant 图image

羊角面包
croissant

面包卷
bread roll

面包
bread

烤面包
toast

饼干
biscuits

黄油
butter

凝乳
curd

蛋糕
cake

蛋
egg

煎蛋
fried egg

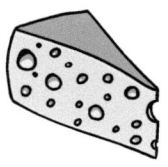

奶酪
cheese

冰激凌

ice cream

糖

sugar

蜂蜜

honey

果酱

jam

巧克力酱

chocolate spread

咖喱饭

curry

农场

farm

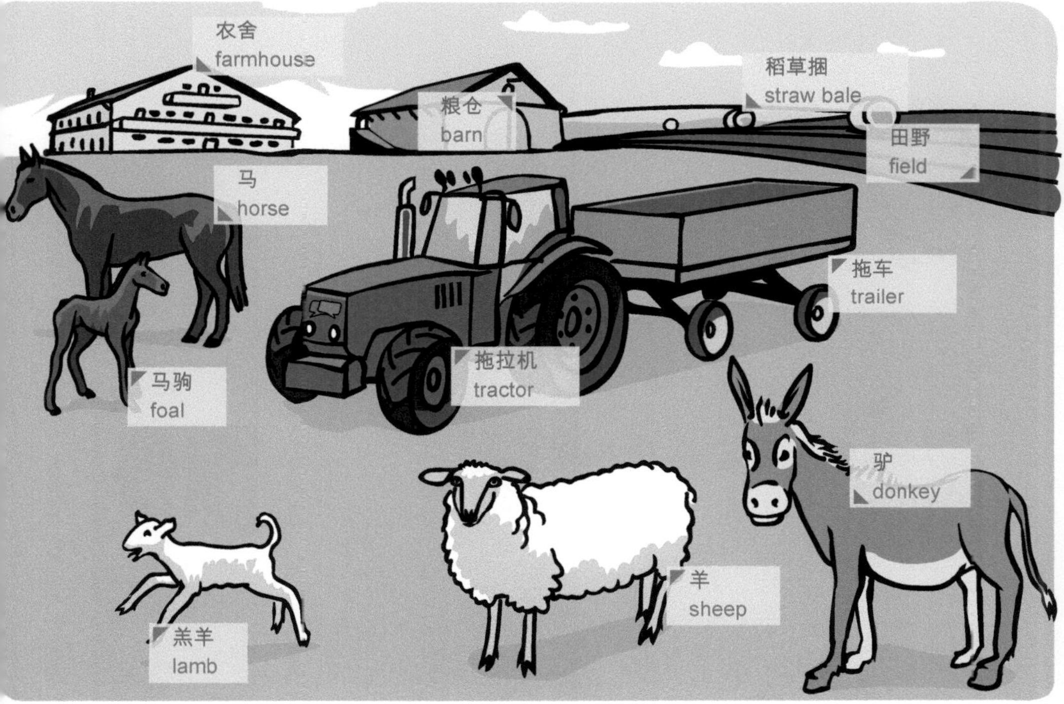

农舍
farmhouse
粮仓
barn
稻草捆
straw bale
田野
field
马
horse
拖车
trailer
马驹
foal
拖拉机
tractor
驴
donkey
羊
sheep
羔羊
lamb

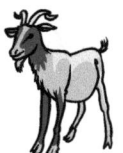

山羊

goat

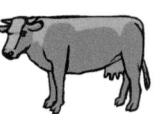

奶牛

cow

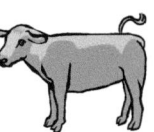

牛犊

calf

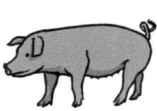

猪

pig

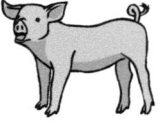

小猪

piglet

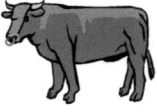

公牛

bull

鹅
goose

鸭
duck

小鸡
chick

母鸡
hen

公鸡
cock

鼠
rat

猫
cat

老鼠
mouse

牛
ox

狗
dog

狗屋
doghouse

花园浇水软管
garden hose

洒水壶
watering can

长柄大镰刀
scythe

犁
plough

镰刀
sickle

锄头
hoe

长柄草耙
pitchfork

斧头
axe

独轮手推车
wheelbarrow

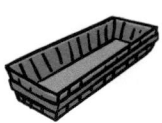

饲料槽
trough

牛奶罐
milk can

麻布袋
sack

栅栏
fence

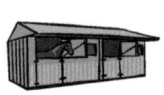

马厩
stable

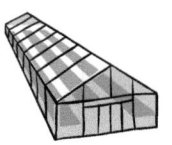

温室
greenhouse

土壤
soil

种子
seed

肥料
fertilizer

联合收割机
combine harvester

农场 - farm

收割

harvest

收割

harvest

山药

yams

小麦

wheat

大豆

soy

土豆

potato

玉米

corn

油菜籽

rapeseed

果树

fruit tree

树薯

cassava

谷物

cereals

房子

house

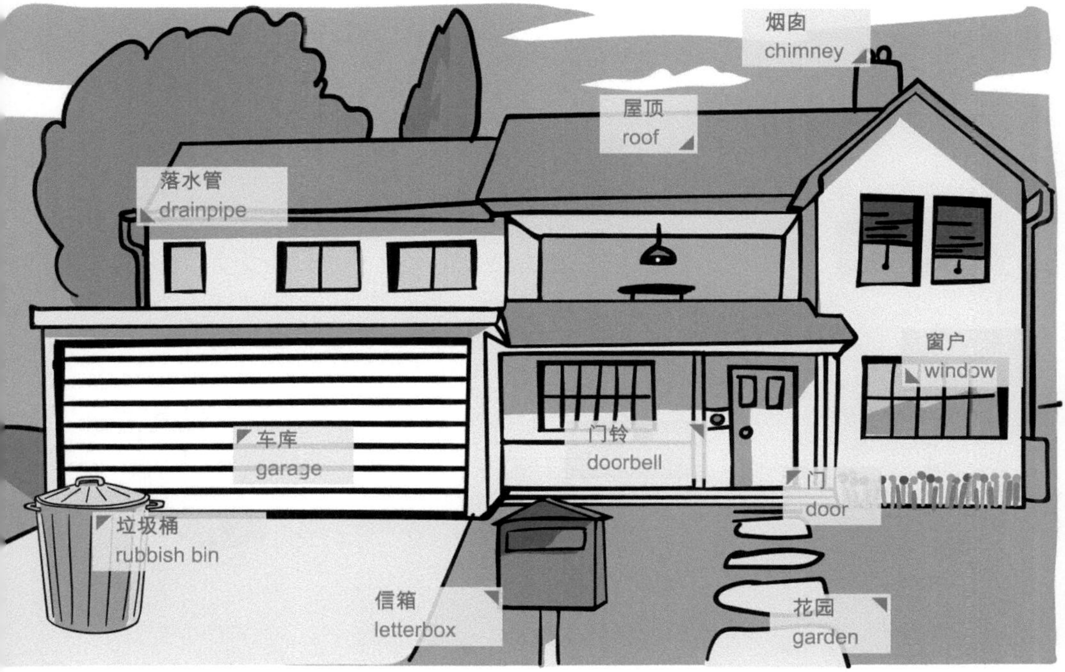

烟囱
chimney
屋顶
roof
落水管
drainpipe
窗户
window
车库
garage
门铃
doorbell
门
door
垃圾桶
rubbish bin
信箱
letterbox
花园
garden

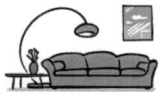

客厅

living room

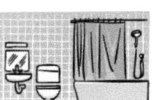

浴室

bathroom

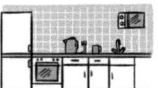

厨房

kitchen

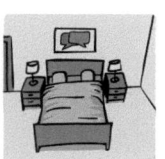

卧室

bedroom

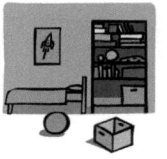

儿童房

child's room

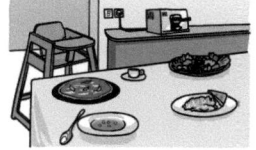

餐厅

dining room

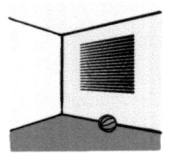

地板

floor

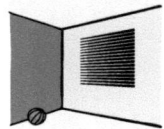

墙壁

wall

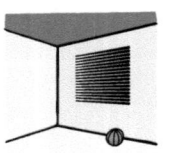

吊顶

ceiling

地窖

cellar

桑拿

sauna

阳台

balcony

露台

terrace

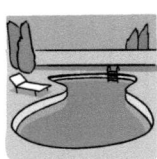

游泳池

pool

割草机

lawn mower

被单

sheet

床罩

bedspread

床

bed

扫帚

broom

水桶

bucket

开关

switch

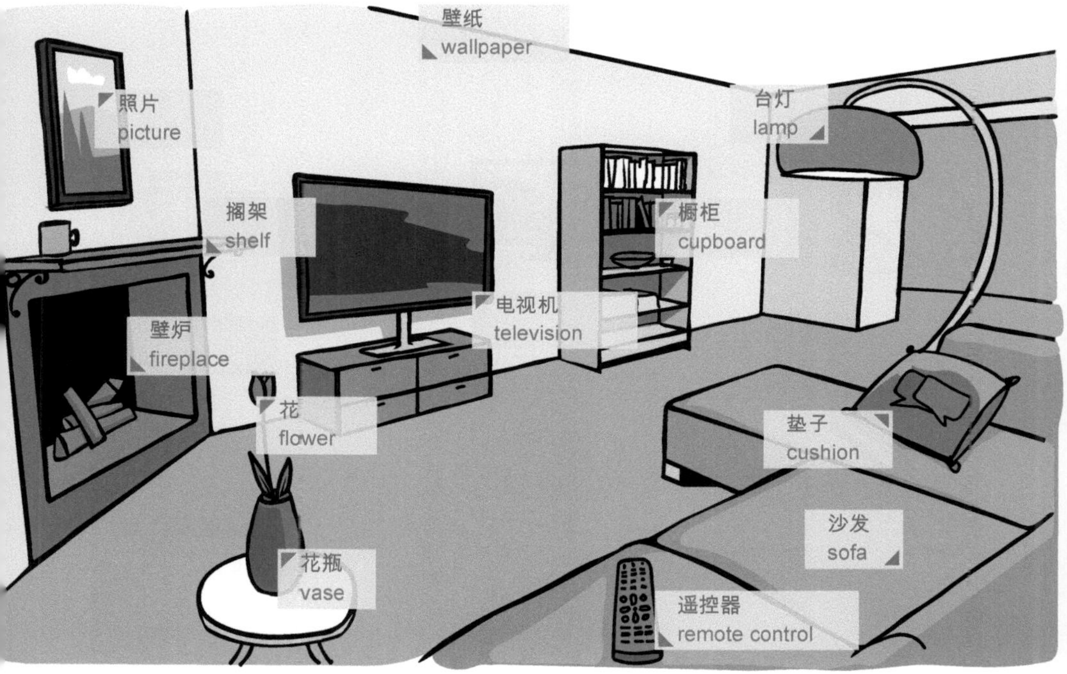

壁纸
wallpaper

照片
picture

台灯
lamp

搁架
shelf

橱柜
cupboard

壁炉
fireplace

电视机
television

花
flower

垫子
cushion

花瓶
vase

沙发
sofa

遥控器
remote control

地毯
carpet

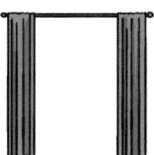

窗帘
curtain

餐桌
table

椅子
chair

摇椅
rocking chair

扶手椅
armchair

书

book

毯子

blanket

装饰品

decoration

木柴

firewood

电影

film

高保真音响

hi-fi equipment

钥匙

key

报纸

newspaper

油画

painting

海报

poster

收音机

radio

笔记本

notepad

吸尘器

hoover

仙人掌

cactus

蜡烛

candle

厨房
kitchen

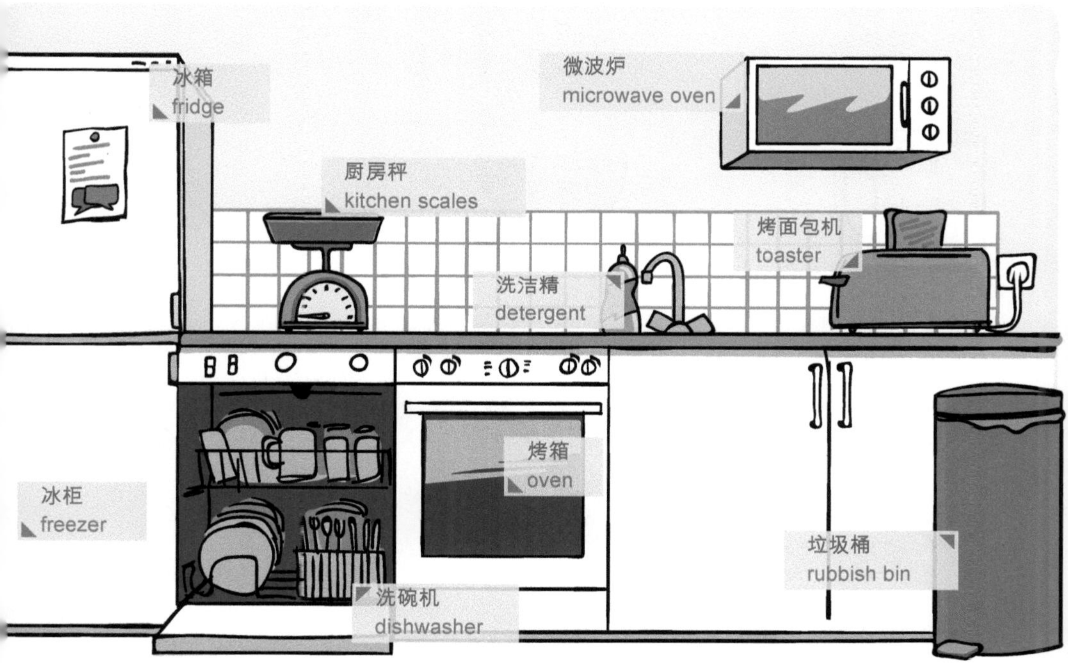
冰箱
fridge
微波炉
microwave oven
厨房秤
kitchen scales
烤面包机
toaster
洗洁精
detergent
烤箱
oven
冰柜
freezer
垃圾桶
rubbish bin
洗碗机
dishwasher

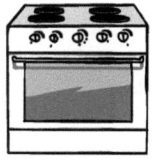

炊具
cooker

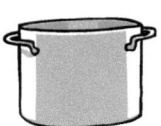

锅
pot

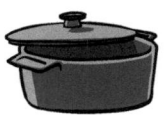

铸铁锅
cast-iron pot

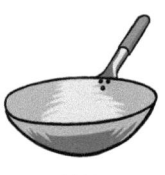

炒锅
wok / kadai

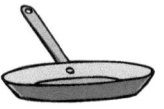

平底锅
pan

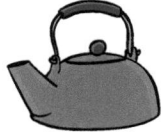

水壶
kettle

蒸锅

steamer

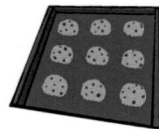

烤盘

baking tray

陶瓷锅

crockery

马克杯

mug

碗

bowl

筷子

chopsticks

长柄勺

ladle

铲子

spatula

搅拌器

whisk

滤网

strainer

筛子

sieve

磨碎机

grater

研钵

mortar

烧烤

barbecue

明火

open fire

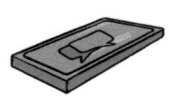

菜板
chopping board

擀面杖
rolling pin

开瓶器
corkscrew

罐子
can

开罐器
can opener

隔热手套
pot holder

水槽
sink

刷子
brush

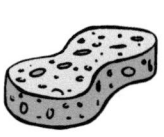

海绵
sponge

搅拌机
blender

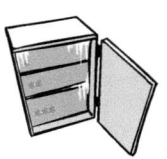

冷藏箱
deep freezer

奶瓶
baby bottle

水龙头
tap

浴室
bathroom

供暖设备
heating

淋浴
shower

毛巾
towel

浴帘
shower curtain

泡沫浴
bubble bath

浴缸
bathtub

玻璃杯
glass

洗衣机
washing machine

瓷砖
tiles

水龙头
tap

便壶
potty

水槽
sink

厕所
toilet

蹲便器
squat toilet

坐浴器
bidet

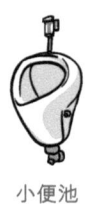

小便池
urinal

厕纸
toilet paper

马桶刷
toilet brush

牙刷
toothbrush

牙膏
toothpaste

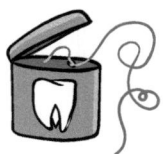

牙线
dental floss

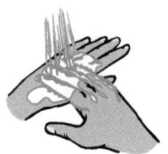

洗
wash

手持式喷淋头
handheld shower

冲洗器
douche

洗脸盆
basin

擦背刷
back brush

肥皂
soap

沐浴露
shower gel

洗发水
shampoo

法兰绒
flannel

排水
drain

乳霜
cream

除臭剂
deodorant

浴室 - bathroom

镜子

mirror

手镜

hand mirror

剃须刀

razor

剃须泡沫

shaving foam

须后水

aftershave

梳子

comb

刷子

brush

吹风机

hair dryer

喷发定型剂

hairspray

化妆品

makeup

唇膏

lipstick

指甲油

nail varnish

化妆棉

cotton wool

指甲剪

nail scissors

香水

perfume

洗漱包

washbag

凳子

stool

计重秤

weighing scale

浴袍

bathrobe

橡胶手套

rubber gloves

卫生棉条

tampon

卫生巾

sanitary towel

化学厕所

chemical toilet

儿童房

child's room

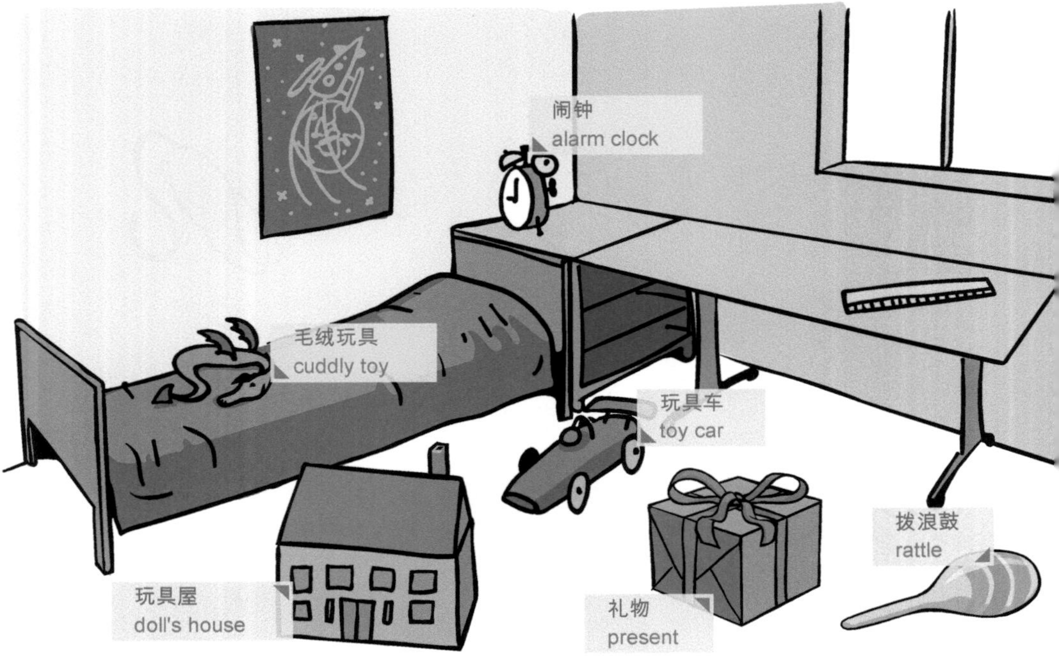
闹钟
alarm clock
毛绒玩具
cuddly toy
玩具车
toy car
拨浪鼓
rattle
玩具屋
doll's house
礼物
present

气球

balloon

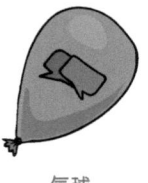

床

bed

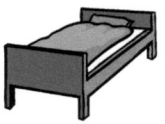

（洋娃娃用）婴儿车

pram

扑克牌

deck of cards

拼图

jigsaw

SUPER MEGA

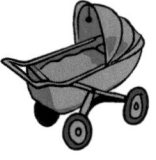

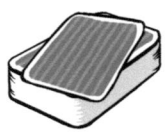

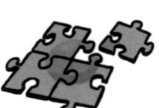

漫画

comic

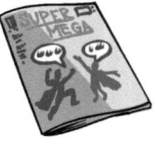

乐高积木

lego bricks

积木玩具

building blocks

玩具人

action figure

婴儿服

babygrow

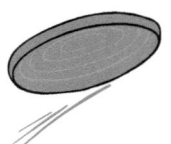

飞盘

frisbee

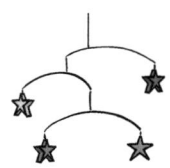

床铃玩具

mobile

棋盘游戏

board game

骰子

dice

火车模型

model train set

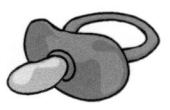

安抚奶嘴

dummy

聚会

party

绘本

picture book

球

ball

洋娃娃

doll

玩

play

儿童房 - child's room

沙坑

sandpit

秋千

swing

玩具

toys

游戏机

video game console

三轮车

tricycle

泰迪熊

teddy bear

衣柜

wardrobe

衣服
clothing

袜子

socks

长袜

stockings

紧身裤

tights

围巾
scarf

雨伞
umbrella

T恤
t-shirt

皮带
belt

靴子
boots

拖鞋
slippers

运动鞋
trainers

凉鞋
sandals

鞋
shoes

雨靴
rubber boots

内裤
underpants

胸罩
bra

背心
vest

衣服 - clothing

45

身体

body

裤子

trousers

牛仔裤

jeans

短裙

skirt

女式衬衫

blouse

衬衫

shirt

套头衫

pullover

卫衣

hoodie

西装夹克

blazer

夹克

jacket

外套

coat

雨衣

raincoat

套装

costume

连衣裙

dress

婚纱

wedding dress

西装
suit

睡袍
nightgown

睡衣
pyjamas

莎丽
sari

头巾
headscarf

包头巾
turban

波卡
burqa

卡夫坦
kaftan

(阿拉伯式)长袍
abaya

泳衣
swimsuit

男式泳裤
trunks

短裤
shorts

运动服
tracksuit

围裙
apron

手套
gloves

纽扣

button

眼镜

glasses

手链

bracelet

项链

necklace

戒指

ring

耳环

earring

便帽

cap

衣架

coat hanger

帽子

hat

领带

tie

拉链

zip

头盔

helmet

背带

braces

校服

school uniform

制服

uniform

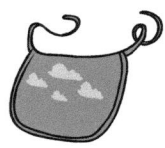

围兜

bib

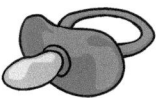

安抚奶嘴

dummy

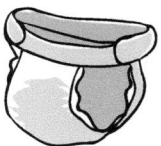

尿不湿

nappy

办公室
office

服务器
server
文件柜
filing cabinet
打印机
printer
纸
paper
显示屏
monitor
鼠标
mouse
办公桌
desk
文件夹
folder
键盘
keyboard
废纸筐
waste-paper basket
电脑
computer
椅子
chair

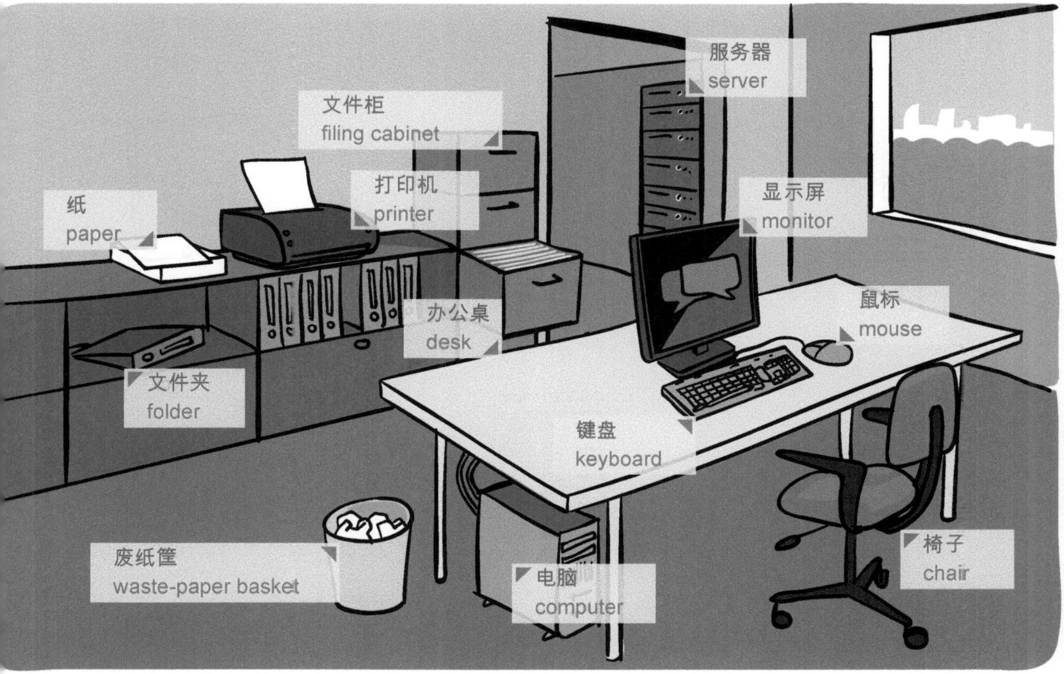

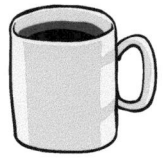

咖啡杯

coffee mug

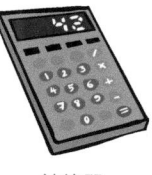

计算器

calculator

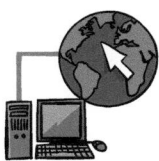

因特网

internet

笔记本电脑
laptop

信件
letter

消息
message

手机
mobile

网络
network

复印机
photocopier

软件
software

电话
telephone

插座
plug socket

传真机
fax machine

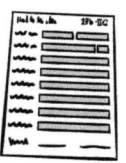

表格
form

文件
document

买

buy

付钱

pay

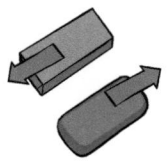

交易

trade

现金

money

美元

dollar

欧元

euro

日元

yen

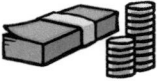

卢布

rouble

瑞士法郎

Swiss franc

人民币

renminbi yuan

卢比

rupee

提款处

cashpoint

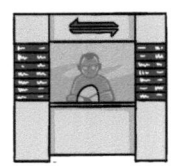

外币兑换处

bureau de change

金

gold

银

silver

石油

oil

能源

energy

价格

price

合同

contract

税金

tax

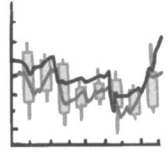

股票

stock

工作

work

职员

employee

老板

employer

工厂

factory

商店

shop

职业

occupations

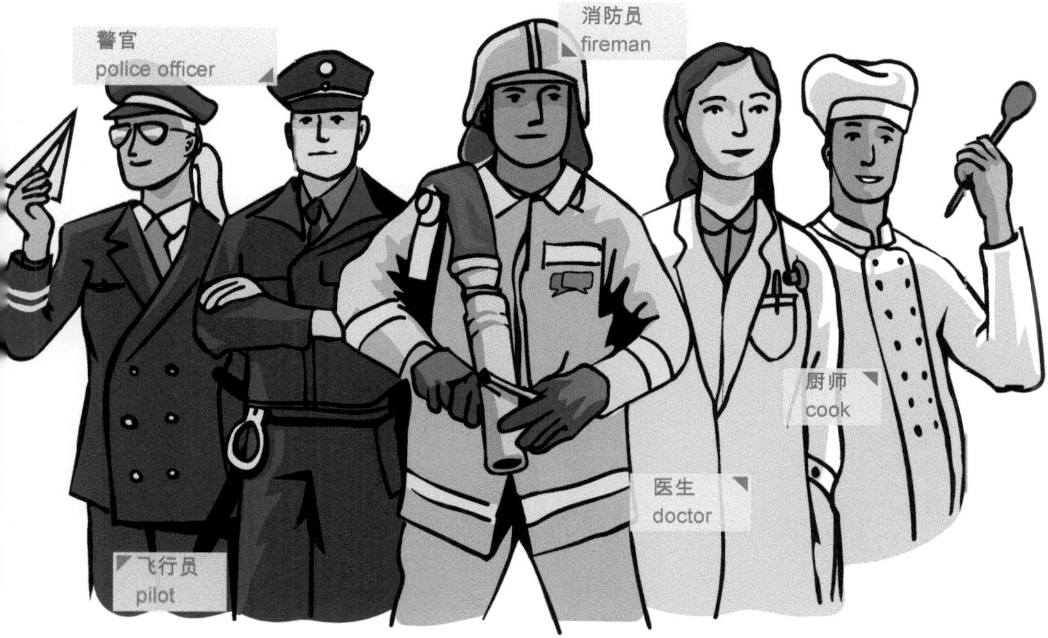
警官
police officer
消防员
fireman
厨师
cook
医生
doctor
飞行员
pilot

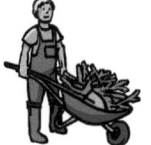

园丁

gardener

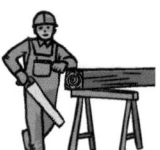

木匠

carpenter

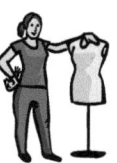

裁缝

seamstress

法官

judge

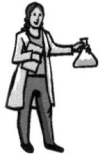

化学家

chemist

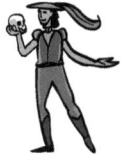

演员

actor

公交车司机

bus driver

出租车司机

taxi driver

渔夫

fisherman

清洁女工

cleaning lady

屋顶工

roofer

服务员

waiter

猎人

hunter

画家

painter

面包师

baker

电工

electrician

建筑工人

builder

工程师

engineer

屠夫

butcher

水管工

plumber

邮递员

postman

士兵

soldier

建筑师

architect

收银员

cashier

花农

florist

理发师

hairdresser

售票员

conductor

机械师

mechanic

船长

captain

牙医

dentist

科学家

scientist

拉比

rabbi

伊玛目

imam

和尚

monk

牧师

clergyman

工具

tools

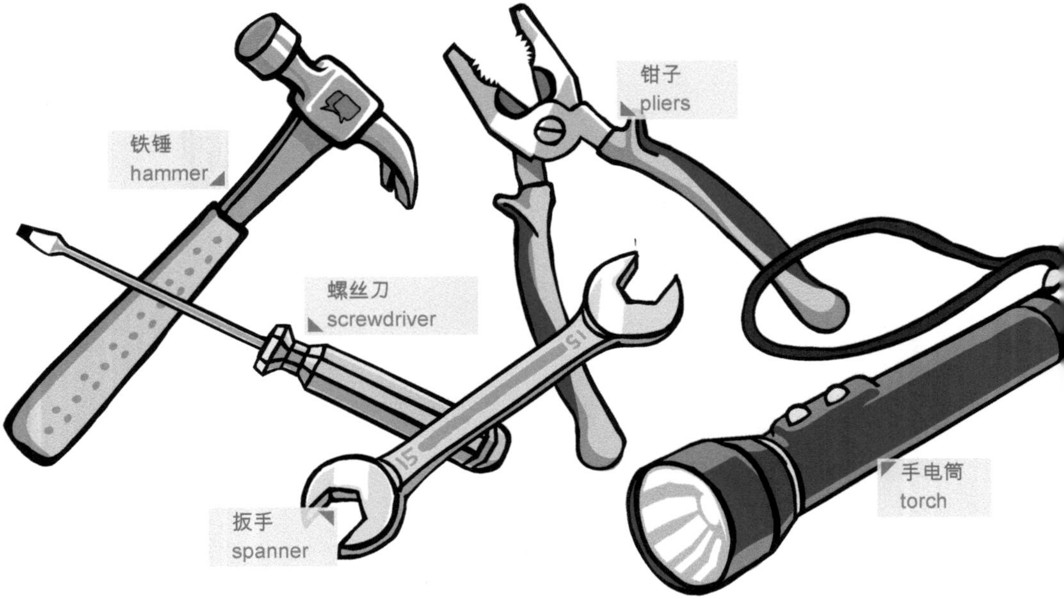
钳子
pliers
铁锤
hammer
螺丝刀
screwdriver
扳手
spanner
手电筒
torch

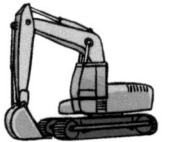

挖掘机
digger

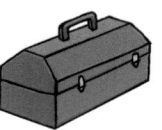

工具箱
toolbox

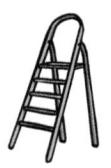

梯子
ladder

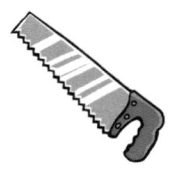

锯子
saw

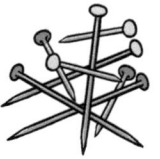

钉子
nails

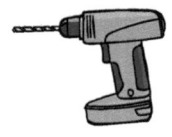

钻机
drill

修
repair

铲子
shovel

靠！
Damn!

簸箕
dustpan

油漆桶
paint pot

螺丝
screws

乐器
musical instruments

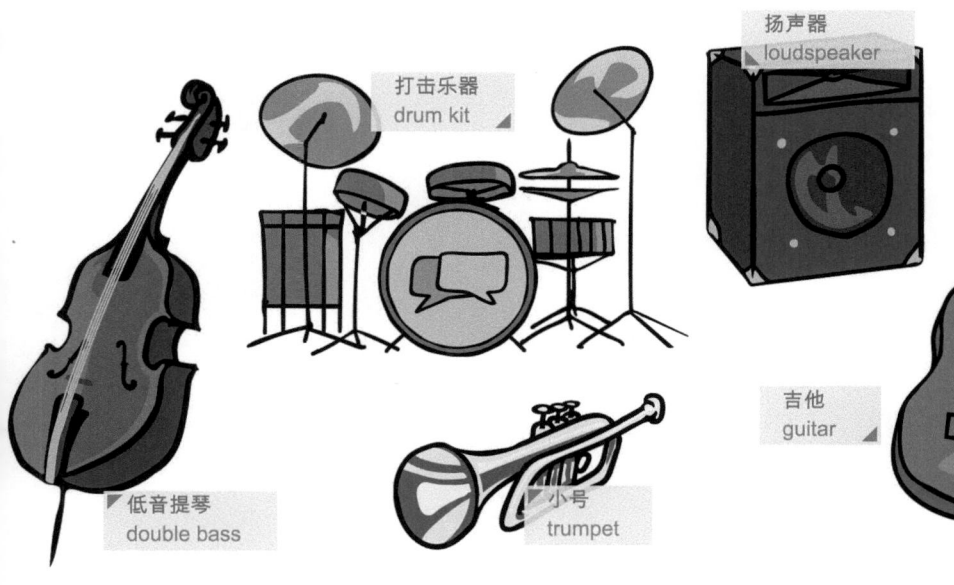

扬声器
loudspeaker

打击乐器
drum kit

吉他
guitar

低音提琴
double bass

小号
trumpet

钢琴

piano

小提琴

violin

贝斯

bass

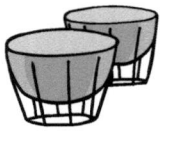

定音鼓

timpani

鼓

drums

电子琴

keyboard

萨克斯管

saxophone

长笛

flute

麦克风

microphone

乐器 - musical instruments

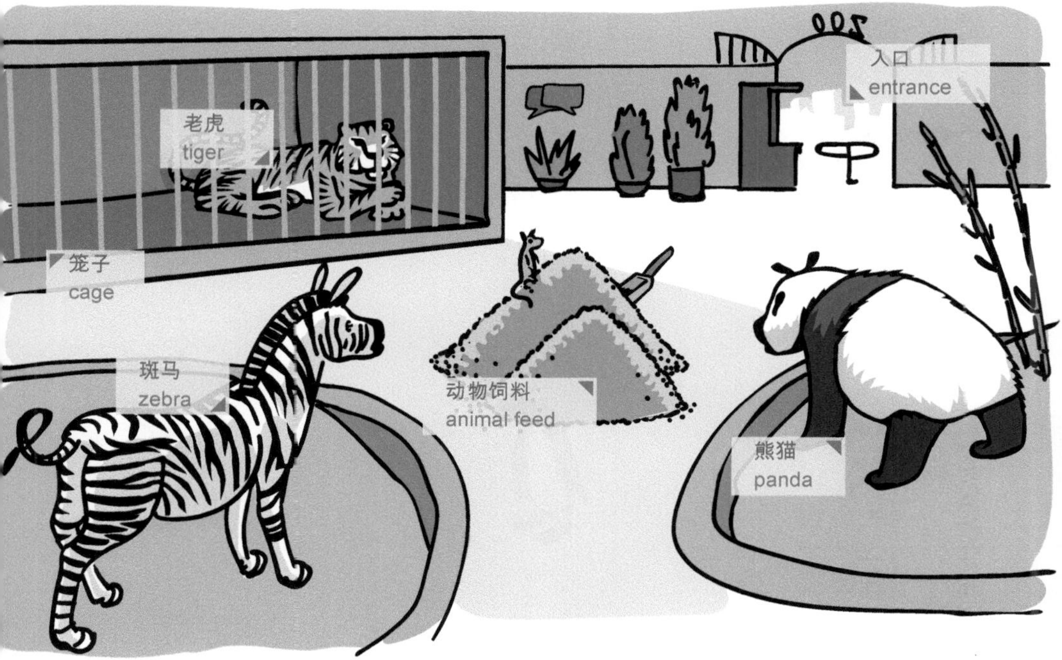

老虎
tiger

入口
entrance

笼子
cage

斑马
zebra

动物饲料
animal feed

熊猫
panda

动物
animals

大象
elephant

袋鼠
kangaroo

犀牛
rhino

大猩猩
gorilla

熊
bear

骆驼

camel

鸵鸟

ostrich

狮子

lion

猴子

monkey

火烈鸟

flamingo

鹦鹉

parrot

北极熊

polar bear

企鹅

penguin

鲨鱼

shark

孔雀

peacock

蛇

snake

鳄鱼

crocodile

动物园管理员

zookeeper

海豹

seal

美洲豹

jaguar

矮种马

pony

豹

leopard

河马

hippo

长颈鹿

giraffe

老鹰

eagle

野猪

boar

鱼

fish

龟

turtle

海象

walrus

狐狸

fox

羚羊

gazelle

橄榄球
American football

骑自行车
cycling

网球
tennis

篮球
basketball

游泳
swimming

拳击
boxing

冰球
ice hockey

英式足球
football

羽毛球
badminton

田径
athletics

手球
handball

滑雪
skiing

马球
polo

跳
jump

笑
laugh

拥抱
hug

唱
sing

走路
walk

做梦
dream

祈祷
pray

亲吻
kiss

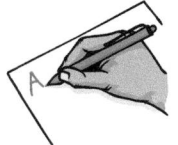

书写
write

画
draw

展示
show

推
push

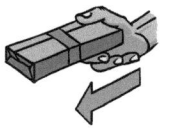

给
give

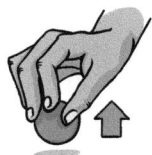

拿
take

活动 - activities

有
have

做
do

当
be

站
stand

跑
run

拉
pull

扔
throw

摔倒
fall

躺
lie

等待
wait

携带
carry

坐
sit

穿衣
get dressed

睡觉
sleep

醒来
wake up

看
look at

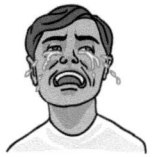

哭
cry

抚摸
stroke

梳头
comb

交谈
talk

明白
understand

问
ask

听
listen

喝
drink

吃
eat

清理
tidy up

爱
love

做饭
cook

开车
drive

飞
fly

活动 - activities

航行

sail

计算

calculate

读

read

学习

learn

工作

work

结婚

marry

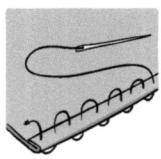

缝

sew

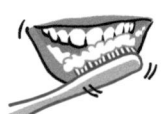

刷牙

brush teeth

杀

kill

抽烟

smoke

寄

send

家

family

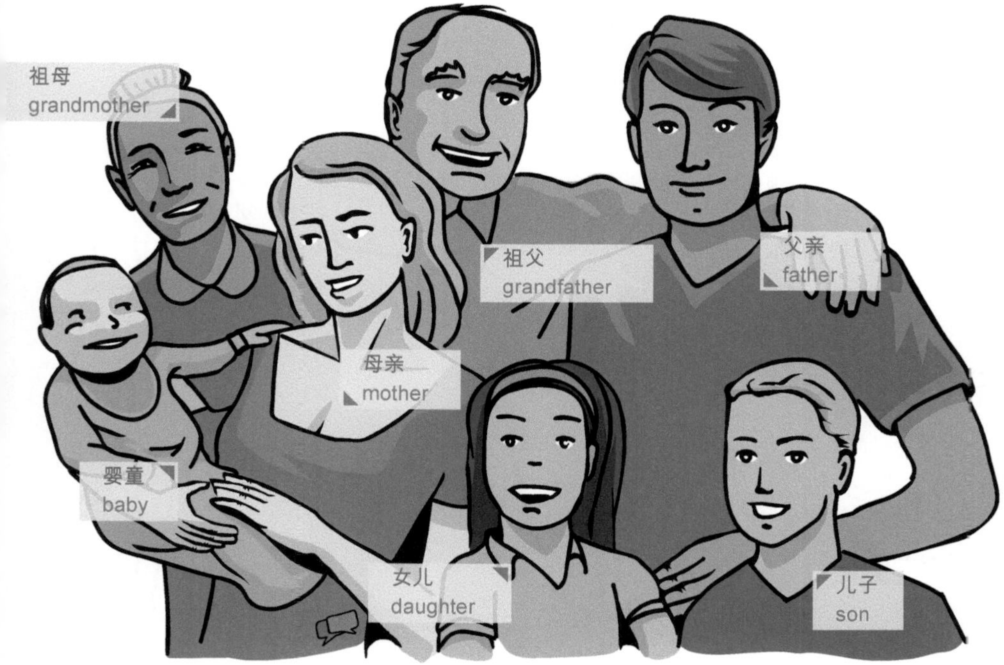

祖母
grandmother
祖父
grandfather
父亲
father
母亲
mother
婴童
baby
女儿
daughter
儿子
son

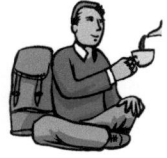

客人

guest

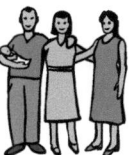

阿姨

aunt

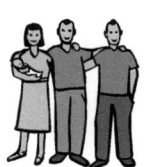

叔叔

uncle

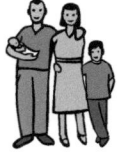

兄弟

brother

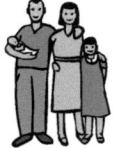

姐妹

sister

身体

body

前额
forehead
眼睛
eye
肩膀
shoulder
手指
finger
脸
face
下巴
chin
手
hand
腿
leg
乳房
breast
手臂
arm

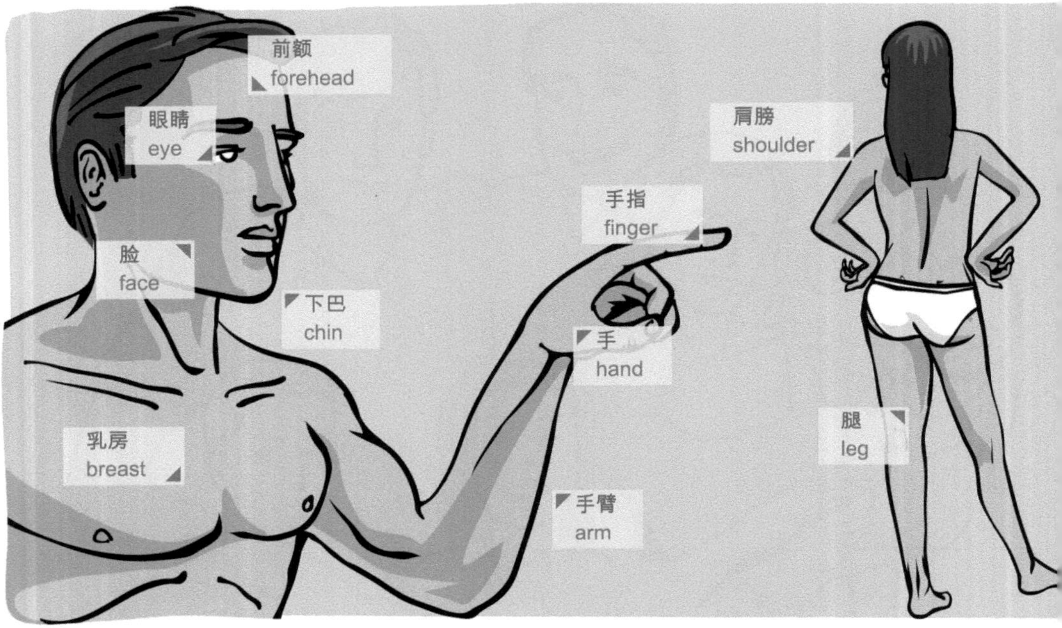

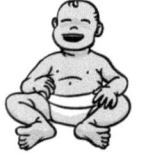

婴童

baby

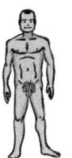

男人

man

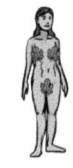

女人

woman

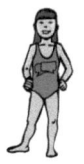

女孩

girl

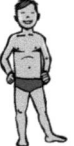

男孩

boy

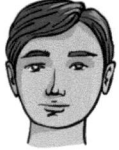

头

head

背部

back

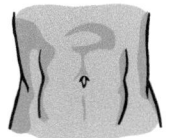

肚子

belly

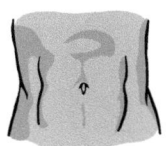

肚脐

belly button

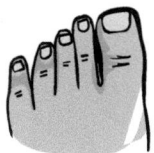

脚趾

toe

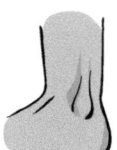

脚后跟

heel

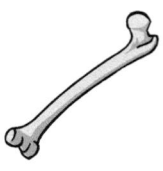

骨头

bone

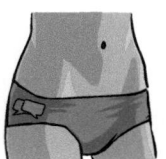

臀部

hip

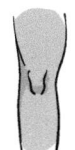

膝盖

knee

手肘

elbow

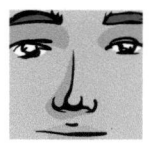

鼻子

nose

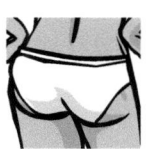

屁股

bottom

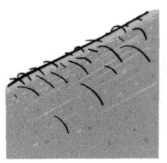

皮肤

skin

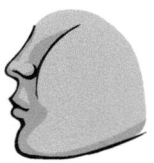

脸颊

cheek

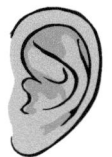

耳朵

ear

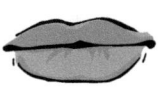

嘴唇

lip

身体 - body

嘴
mouth

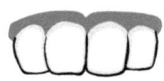

牙齿
tooth

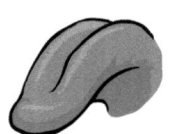

舌头
tongue

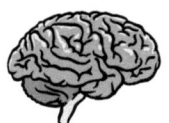

脑
brain

心脏
heart

肌肉
muscle

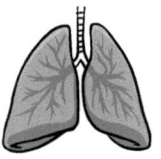

肺
lung

肝脏
liver

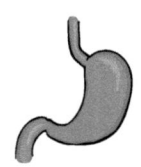

胃
stomach

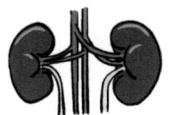

肾脏
kidneys

性交
sex

避孕套
condom

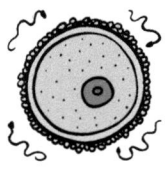

卵子
ovum

精子
semen

怀孕
pregnancy

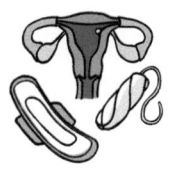

月经

menstruation

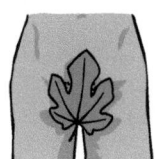

阴道

vagina

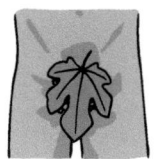

阴茎

penis

眉毛

eyebrow

头发

hair

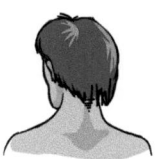

脖子

neck

医院
hospital

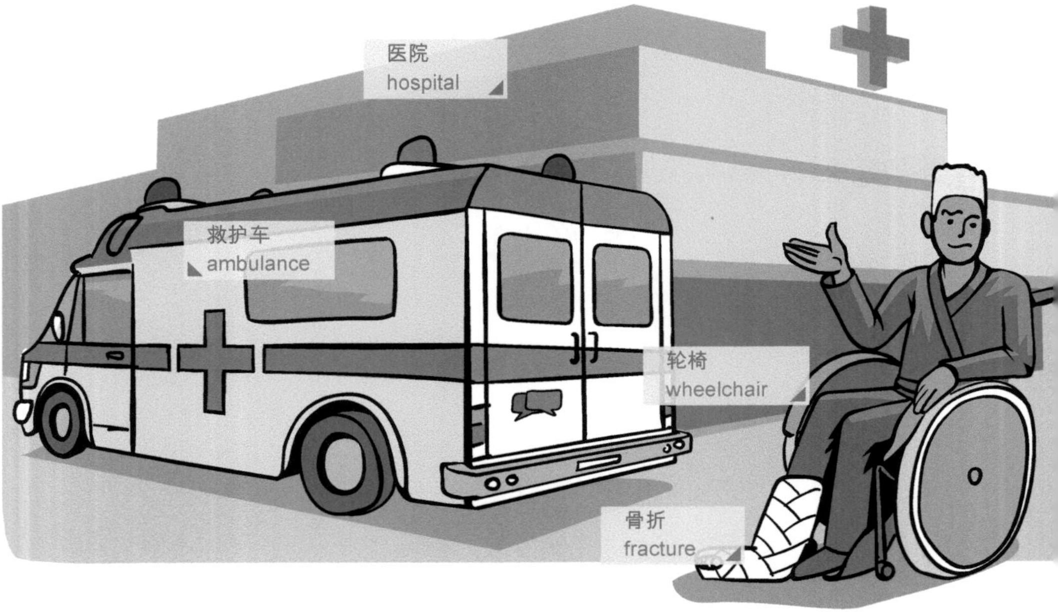

医院
hospital
救护车
ambulance
轮椅
wheelchair
骨折
fracture

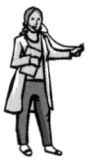

医生

doctor

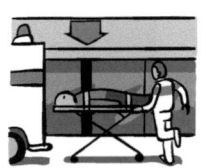

急诊室

emergency room

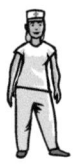

护士

nurse

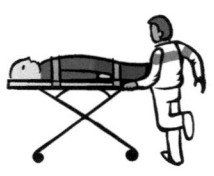

紧急情况

emergency

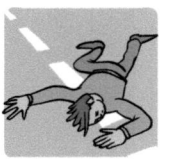

昏迷

unconscious

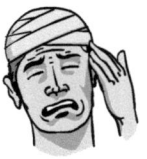

痛

pain

受伤

injury

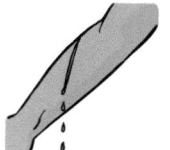

出血

bleeding

心脏病发作

heart attack

中风

stroke

过敏

allergy

咳嗽

cough

发烧

fever

流感

flu

腹泻

diarrhoea

头痛

headache

癌症

cancer

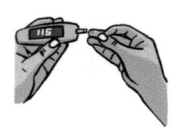

糖尿病

diabetes

外科医生

surgeon

手术刀

scalpel

手术

operation

CT

CT

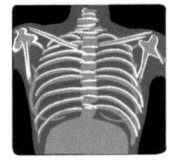

X光

x-ray

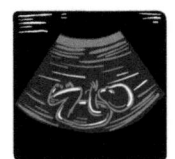

超声波

ultrasound

口罩

face mask

疾病

disease

候诊室

waiting room

拐杖

crutch

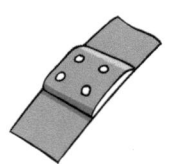

石膏

plaster

绷带

bandage

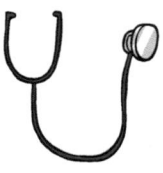

注射

injection

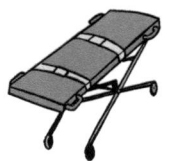

听诊器

stethoscope

担架

stretcher

体温计

clinical thermometer

出生

birth

超重

overweight

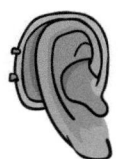

助听器

hearing aid

消毒液

disinfectant

感染

infection

病毒

virus

艾滋病

HIV / AIDS

药物

medicine

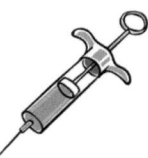

接种疫苗

vaccination

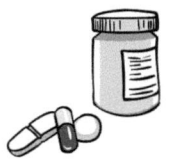

药片

tablets

药丸

pill

急救电话

emergency call

血压计

blood pressure monitor

生病/健康

ill / healthy

救命！
Help!

警报
alarm

突击
assault

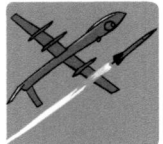

攻击
attack

危险
danger

紧急出口
emergency exit

着火啦！
Fire!

灭火器
fire extinguisher

意外
accident

急救箱
first-aid kit

呼救信号
SOS

警察
police

欧洲

Europe

北美洲

North America

南美洲

South America

非洲

Africa

亚洲

Asia

澳洲

Australia

大西洋

Atlantic

太平洋

Pacific

印度洋

Indian Ocean

南冰洋

Antarctic Ocean

北冰洋

Arctic Ocean

北极

North Pole

南极

South Pole

南极洲

Antarctica

地球

Earth

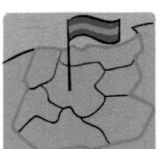

陆地

land

海

sea

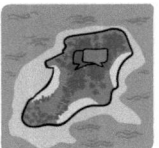

岛

island

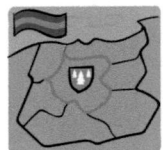

国家

nation

国家

state

钟面

clock face

时针

hour hand

分针

minute hand

秒针

second hand

现在几点？

What time is it?

天

day

时间

time

现在

now

电子表

digital watch

分

minute

时

hour

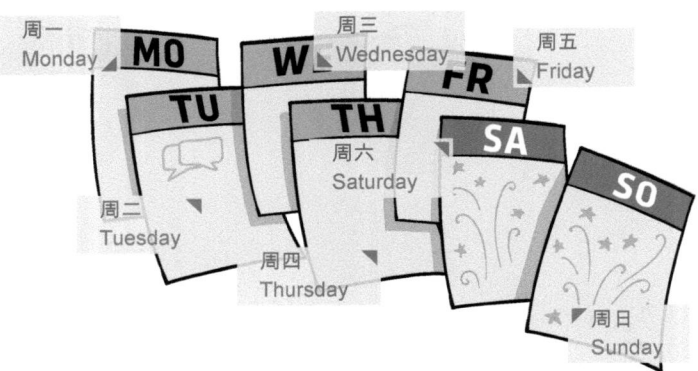

周一 Monday
周三 Wednesday
周五 Friday
周二 Tuesday
周六 Saturday
周四 Thursday
周日 Sunday

昨天

yesterday

今天

today

明天

tomorrow

早晨

morning

中午

noon

晚上

evening

工作日

business days

周末

weekend

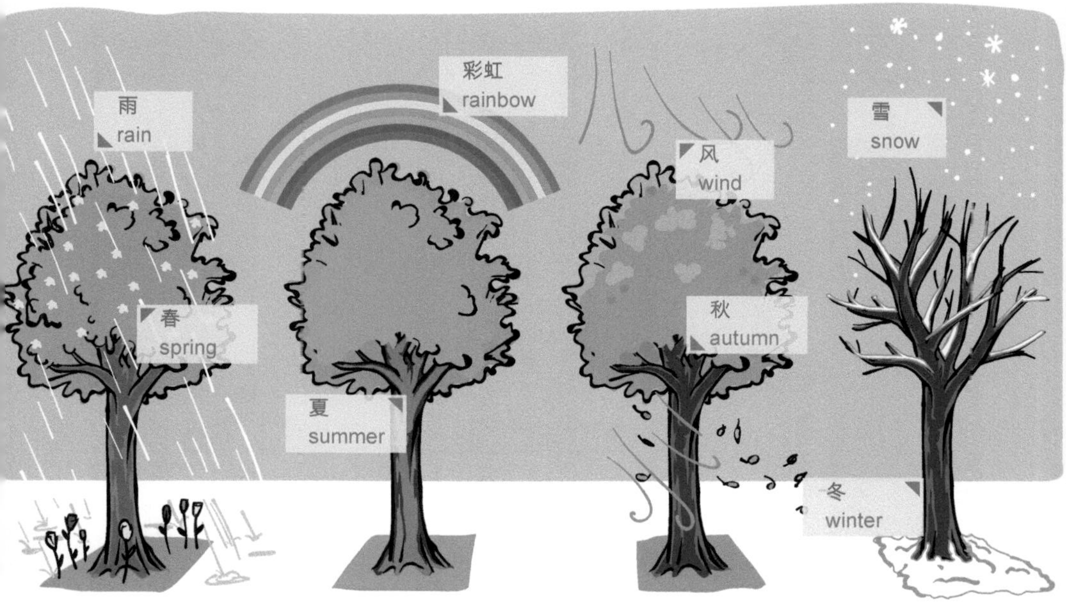
雨
rain
彩虹
rainbow
风
wind
雪
snow
春
spring
夏
summer
秋
autumn
冬
winter

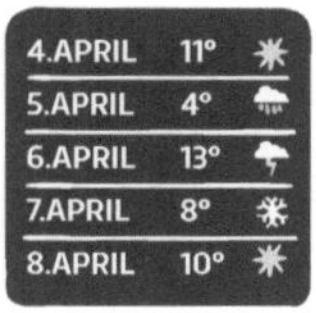
4.APRIL 11°
5.APRIL 4°
6.APRIL 13°
7.APRIL 8°
8.APRIL 10°

天气预报

weather forecast

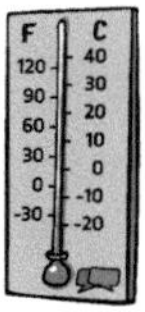
F
C
120
90
60
30
0
-30
40
30
20
10
0
-10
-20

温度计

thermometer

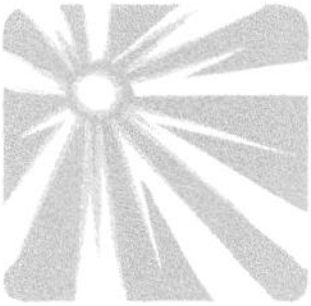

阳光

sunshine

云

cloud

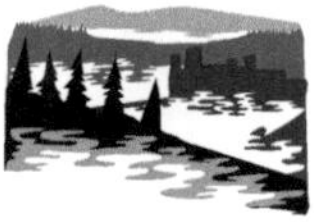

雾

fog

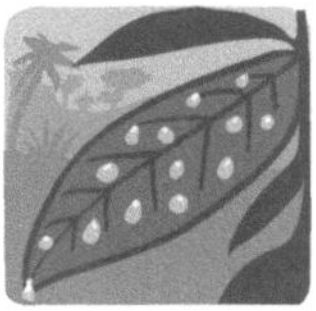

潮湿

humidity

闪电

lightning

打雷

thunder

风暴

storm

冰雹

hail

季风

monsoon

洪水

flood

冰

ice

一月

January

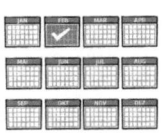

二月

February

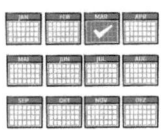

三月

March

四月

April

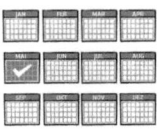

五月

May

六月

June

七月

July

八月

August

年 - year

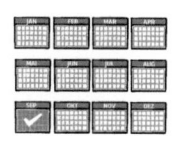

九月

September

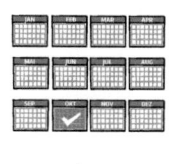

十月

October

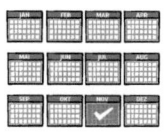

十一月

November

十二月

December

形状
shapes

圆形

circle

正方形

square

长方形

rectangle

三角形

triangle

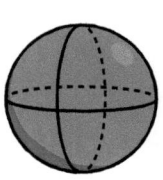

球体

sphere

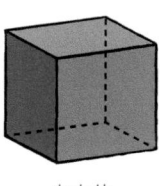

立方体

cube

白
white

黄
yellow

橙
orange

粉
pink

红
red

紫
purple

蓝
blue

绿
green

棕
brown

灰
grey

黑
black

很多/少许

a lot / a little

生气/平静

angry / calm

美/丑

beautiful / ugly

首/尾

beginning / end

大/小

big / small

明/暗

bright / dark

兄弟/姐妹

brother / sister

干净/肮脏

clean / dirty

完整/缺失

complete / incomplete

白天/晚上

day / night

死/生

dead / alive

宽/窄

wide / narrow

可食用/非食用

edible / inedible

邪恶/善良

evil / kind

兴奋/无聊

excited / bored

胖/瘦

fat / thin

第一/最后

first / last

朋友/敌人

friend / enemy

满/空

full / empty

硬/软

hard / soft

重/轻

heavy / light

饿/渴

hunger / thirst

生病/健康

ill / healthy

非法/合法

illegal / legal

聪明/愚笨

intelligent / stupid

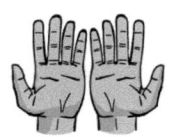

左/右

left / right

近/远

near / far

新/旧
new / used

没有/有些
nothing / something

老/幼
old / young

开/关
on / off

打开/合上
open / closed

安静/吵闹
quiet / loud

富/穷
rich / poor

对/错
right / wrong

粗糙/光滑
rough / smooth

伤心/高兴
sad / happy

短/长
short / long

慢/快
slow / fast

湿/干
wet / dry

温暖/凉爽
warm / cool

战争/和平
war / peace

反义词 - opposites

数字

numbers

0

零
....
zero

1

一
....
one

2

二
....
two

3

三
....
three

4

四
....
four

5

五
....
five

6

六
....
six

7

七
....
seven

8

八
....
eight

9

九
....
nine

10

十
....
ten

11

十一
....
eleven

12
十二
twelve

13
十三
thirteen

14
十四
fourteen

15
十五
fifteen

16
十六
sixteen

17
十七
seventeen

18
十八
eighteen

19
十九
nineteen

20
二十
twenty

100
百
hundred

1.000
千
thousand

1.000.000
百万
million

英语

English

美式英语

American English

普通话

Chinese Mandarin

印地语

Hindi

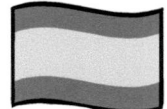

西班牙语

Spanish

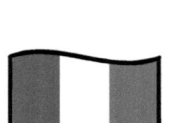

法语

French

阿拉伯语

Arabic

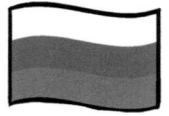

俄语

Russian

葡萄牙语

Portuguese

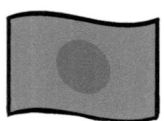

孟加拉语

Bengali

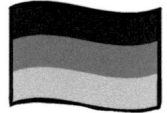

德语

German

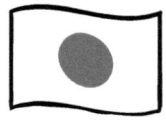

日语

Japanese

我

I

你

you

他/她/它

he / she / it

我们

we

你们

you

他们

they

谁？

who?

什么？

what?

怎样？

how?

哪里？

where?

什么时候？

when?

名字

name

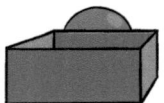

后面

behind

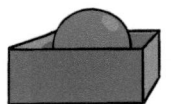

里面

in

前面

in front of

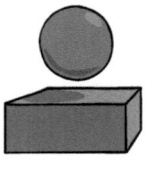

上方

over

上面

on

下面

under

旁边

beside

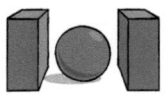

中间

between

地点

place